THE WORLD'S ROOM

P H O E N I X **POETS**

A SERIES EDITED BY ALAN SHAPIRO

JOSHUA WEINER

Joshua Weiner (signature)

the world's room

For Eli, with great pleasure and best wishes for continued luck at the page! All best, Josh

THE UNIVERSITY OF CHICAGO PRESS

Chicago and London

Rome "/25/03

JOSHUA WEINER's work has appeared in *The American Scholar, Best American Poetry, Boston Review, The Nation, Threepenny Review, TriQuarterly,* and *The Village Voice.* Most recently a Witter Bynner Fellow at the Library of Congress, he teaches creative writing and literature at Northwestern University.

The University of Chicago Press, Chicago 60637
The University of Chicago Press, Ltd., London
©2001 by The University of Chicago
All rights reserved. Published 2001
Printed in the United States of America

10 09 08 07 06 05 04 03 02 01   1 2 3 4 5

ISBN 0-226-88575-5 (cloth)
ISBN 0-226-88576-3 (paper)

Library of Congress Cataloging-in-Publication Data
Weiner, Joshua.
    The world's room / Joshua Weiner.
        p.   cm. — (Phoenix poets)
    ISBN 0-226-88575-5 (cloth : alk. paper) —
    ISBN 0-226-88576-3 (paper : alk paper)
    I. Title. II. Series

PS3573.E3937 W67 2001
811'.6—dc21   00-067223

for Sarah

I follow you
    past certainty

And quhat wul ye leive to your bairns and your wife,
                           Edward, Edward?
And quhat wul ye leive to your bairns and your wife,
                           Quhan ye gang ovir the sea, O?
The warldis room, let thame beg throw life,
                           Mither, mither;
The warldis room, let thame beg throw life,
                           For thame nevir mair wul I see, O.

—ANON. SCOTS

Contents

Acknowledgments

I am grateful to the editors of the following periodicals for publishing these poems:

Agni: "Art Pepper," "Nursery Rhyme," "Oakland 1991"
Berkeley Poetry Review: "Mongrel Death Blues"
Boston Phoenix: "Lines to Stitch Inside a Child's Pocket"
Boston Review: "The Not-Yet Child," "The Dog State"
The Forward: "The Visitation," "Psalm"
Harvard Review: "The World's Room"
The Nation: "Overlooking Berkeley"
Threepenny Review: "Market Day," "Who They Were," "Connecting Flight"
Tikkun: "Bruno's Night"
TriQuarterly: "The Knife," *"Kindertotenlieder"*

"Who They Were" was reprinted in *Best American Poetry 1994,* edited by A. R. Ammons and David Lehman (Scribner, 1994). "Bruno's Night" also appeared in *Promotional Copy* (1994) edited by Robin Kahn, and as a video by Bob Paris.

The book's epigraph is from the Anonymous Scots ballad, "Edward, Edward," collected by Thomas Percy in *Reliques of Ancient English Poetry* (1886).

"Plot" is an homage to poet & master carpenter Mark Turpin. One can find his poems in *Nailer,* a book published in a volume of the *Agni New Poets Series, Take Three: 2* (Graywolf, 1997).

"Tempest" identifies the man addressed as Crispus Sallustius, borrowing from Horace's Ode ii.2, translated by David Ferry under the title, "Avarice."

"Kindertotenlieder" (Songs on the Death of Children) takes its title from Gustav Mahler's orchestral accompaniment to the poems of Friedrich Rückert, who wrote his lyrics after two of his children died within a few days of one another.

"Bruno's Night" is inspired by the story "A Night in July" by Bruno Schulz.

The cover image, "The Wondrous Globe," is a photogravure by Annie W. Brigman that originally appeared in *Camera Work 38* (1912).

To Mary Kinzie, first to notice, and Joseph Epstein, first to publish, I owe many thanks. My debt to Thom Gunn and Robert Pinsky is profound, my pleasure in thanking them here more so. XL thanks to Alan Shapiro for his support over many years of revision; it's no exaggeration to say this book would not exist without him. There are many others who have contributed in numerous ways to its completion, and to the completion of individual poems. Thanks, especially, to Frank Bidart, David Gewanter, Reginald Gibbons, Robert Hass, Wendy Lesser, Gail Mazur, Jim Powell, Suzanne Qualls, Claudia Rankine, David Rivard, Tom Sleigh, and Mark Turpin.

Some of these poems were written with support from the Academy of American Poets, the University of California at Berkeley, Dartmouth College, the Fine Arts Work Center in Provincetown, Northwestern University, the San Francisco Foundation, and the Merv Foundation; "Kindertotenlieder" received an Illinois Arts Council Literary Award—thanks to all of them.

Thanks beyond words to my parents, Mervyn Weiner, and Marjorie & Al DeStefano; and to my son, Eli Whitney Blake Weiner, first race-car driver entomologist. There are no adequate thanks for my wife, Sarah Blake, to whom this book is dedicated.

THE WORLD'S ROOM

Psalm

When I sing to you I am alone these days
                and can't believe it, as if the stars

—while gazing up at them—just shut off.
                Astonished:

I search out the one light, brightest light
                in the night sky, but find

I cannot find it without weaker lights to guide me
                like red tail-lights on a car up ahead

after midnight when I'm sleepy, that illustrate
                how the highway curves,

curving to a hook, and maybe save my life
                and it means nothing to me

because nothing has happened, not the faintest
                glint of drama.

(Raining gently, the tarmac turns slick, moistened
                to life with renewed residues;

I can sense it with my hands on the wheel,
                the drops—not too heavy—

drumming off-time rhythms on the metal roof,
           the metal surface like a skin tense and sweating

and the road empty now, there are so many
           exits . . .)

Where is my family, both hearth and constellated trail of flicker
           I have always followed to your word?

There, but mastered by fear of dark compulsions
           and loathing atrocities committed in your name,

they hit the dimmer switch and extinguish themselves
           whenever I sing your praises . . .

Who can blame them?
           (I can't help but blame them.)

And anyway they are far from me
           (farthest when they come to visit)—

I should be self-reliant, in my armchair
           like Emerson reading by a single lamp;

I should not need them, finding in you
           myself, little firebug needing no outlet,

my soft light blinking as I oxidize my aimless flight
           to love, to the good,

even my glowing chemistry unnecessary now
           in the ultimate light of day.

But what good would that do me?
           With you, in you, perhaps others do not matter,

but this isn't heaven, and I cannot make a circle
           all on my own—

Photon, luciferin, meteor: as I burn myself
           to pieces, I only pray

let my sparking tail remain a moment longer
           than our physics might allow,

some indication, however brief, that there continues
           (amen) a path to follow.

The Yonder Tree

Bought myself a ticket, the ticket freed me,
I flew through a storm to the yonder tree.
    I said to myself   *now I can see, now I can see.*

Bought myself a horse, the horse pleased me,
I rode my horse to the yonder tree.
    The horse said   *nay, nay.*
    I said to myself   *now I can see, now I can see.*

Bought myself a cat, the cat pleased me,
I chased that cat to the yonder tree.
    The cat said   *me, me.*
    The horse said   *nay, nay.*
    I said to myself   *now I can see, now I can see.*

Bought myself a dog, the dog pleased me,
I walked my dog to the yonder tree.
    The dog said   *bow down.*
    The cat said   *me, me.*
    The horse said   *nay, nay.*
    I said to myself   *now I can see, now I can see.*

Found myself a woman, the woman pleased me,
I followed my woman to the yonder tree.
    The woman said   *maybe, baby.*
    The dog said   *bow down.*

The cat said   *me, me.*
The horse said   *nay, nay.*
I said to myself   *now I can see, now I can see.*

Bought myself a knife, the knife pleased me,
I cut two names into the yonder tree.
 The knife said   *hungry, angry.*
 The woman said   *maybe, baby.*
 The dog said   *bow down.*
 The cat said   *me, me.*
 The horse said   *nay, nay.*
 I said to myself   *now I can see, now I can see.*

Bought myself a house, the house pleased me,
I built my house from the yonder tree.
 The house said   *comfort, come back.*
 The knife said   *hungry, angry.*
 The woman said   *maybe, baby.*
 The dog said   *bow down.*
 The cat said   *me, me.*
 The horse said   *nay, nay.*
 I said to myself   *now I can see, now I can see.*

Bought myself a watch, the watch pleased me,
I checked my watch at the yonder tree.
 The watch said   *tick, take.*
 The house said   *comfort, come back.*
 The knife said   *hungry, angry.*
 The woman said   *maybe, baby.*
 The dog said   *bow down.*
 The cat said   *me, me.*
 The horse said   *nay, nay.*
 I said to myself   *now I can see, now I can see.*

Bought myself a stone, the stone pleased me,
I placed my stone beneath the yonder tree.

    The stone said   *good-night, this night, all night.*
    The watch said   *tick, take.*
    The house said   *comfort, come back.*
    The knife said   *hungry, angry.*
    The woman said   *maybe, baby.*
    The dog said   *bow down.*
    The cat said   *me, me.*
    The horse said   *nay, nay.*
    I said to myself   *what did I see? I thought I could see . . .*

Overlooking Berkeley

Clear night.
The endless stream
of shivering lights

seems to release
a heat you feel
even this high,

this removed
from sirens, guitars,
a gunning motor.

A shout. Up here
I imagine
in the bright clotted

stream denials
of love, money
exchanged. The moon

hangs like a bell
between hours.
An owl opens

over the drop,
soft-plumed and
silent above

the research lab.
Back on my bike,
pumping further up

the steep incline,
only the sound
of each labored breath,

each revolution
of the crank, the air
a damp whisper.

Musk. From a plant?
At the peak one
poised moment—

then dropping,
the everyday
momentum of the world

pulling me fast
and faster still
down the buckled

hillside, body
tipped toward
the city's braided

excess, its colonies
of scrap, invention,
coded impulse,

the rush itself
a promise beyond
mere falling

past these blind
solicitations:
movies, songs,

fast food,
a few dollars,
her voice vibrating

along the wire
I fly beneath.
I'm tingling, taut

against the bike's
clank and rattle.
I can barely breathe.

The Dog State

Her reproach gathered in my inside atmosphere.
I fantasized my finger
drawing a tear line down her cheek

to trace a trail of hurt I thought to follow.
I hoped to touch her with a lightness
signifying sorrow, with a touch

leading me to sorrow's place
where I could feel it, and in that feeling
compose the man I imagine she loved.

The new dog loved me like a story-book dog,
slept curled tight into a cinnamon bun
by my bed at night, the AC cranked so high

my room was a box of winter inside the heart
of suburban summer heat. She'd wait outside
the houses of friends for hours till I appeared

like a miracle to acknowledge her, to praise
her loyalty, her patience, all sounds emerging
from me sounding like approval

and I did approve, rewarding with my kind attentions.
While working down a bone, she had a way of glancing
up at me, jaws never pausing, and I swear

she was flirting, it made me feel funny
as if she weren't just a dog, the way animals
sometimes express the human—

but like a suggestion it embarrassed me,
having so recently arrived to that year my image
first reflected back as alien and corrupted:

I am enclosed in my own fat, my face scarred;
besides God, who could love me?
And who could I tell what happened,

what might seem just a mindless act
without consequence, like jamming
firecrackers up a frog,

but is only disguised beneath
some hunched and secret purpose,
like waiting to steal

the report card you know will come,
must come as she came
to complement my ugliness:

there in the yard she tensed on a shaggy haunch,
black muzzle moist with slobber,
ears erect, her gaze stitched

to my every movement, the wanting so condensed
her tail sailed without wagging
as I retrieved the bone from beneath the bench

and snapped it back to sling it as far
beyond the yard as I could throw
when she crumpled

cringing beneath the arm now writing this
cocked then to fire without harm.
Not a story-book dog, in fact she was pure mutt

bought cheap from the mailman
who must have beat her often and hard, she cowered
so low to the ground, eye lids fluttering

with fear and acceptance at the human hand
(his knuckles, unlike mine, sprouted hair thick as wire)
preparing to punish without reason.

I felt sick. Why wasn't I destroyed
by my discovery of what I could make her feel
as I raised my hand again to see her sink before me

and again five minutes later.
Like sneaking beer or jerking off,
each time I gestured violence and marveled

as she tried to disappear into the ground,
to become ground yielding enough
to absorb blows that never followed,

it seemed a crime inflicted on
the house I slept in, which kept me cool at night
and sheltered grown-ups still in charge.

A hidden voice whispered cold fury
against me, I had polluted my estate,
and it seemed she heard it too

the day she broke her chain and bolted
down the well-groomed street muted in shade.
Adult sympathy arrived as if on cue, even bellowing

Mr. Shreck, the shop teacher from next door,
lowered his voice to add *I once lost a dog*
in a register I had never before heard him speak;

and they looked at me as if I should know what to do
so I acted sad, it seemed required, hopped on my ten-speed
and set off like John Wayne to search for what I loved.

I slid through a neighborhood broiling with kids
caught in games that could never engage me,
not that day, with my script, *A Boy and His Dog.*

But how could I love
what now lived to shrink from me? She was anywhere
away from me as I circled the driveways

to peek in each backyard, each house
a replica of the house before, each kid recognized
by haircut, height and gait,

connected to a street, parents and a school,
until the catalog of likenesses
collapsed into a single field

sucking into itself everything I was told should matter.
And I thought *New Jersey: The Dog State*—
more dogs than children, cars, or criminals.

The idea of caring had somehow decomposed
although authored by a conscience—
my conscience?—until affection scattered

like an element unleashed by heat.
Soon it would turn dark. Clouds of gnats
thickened. Wanting it to end

I pedaled further into humid green
watching the grown-ups on my mind's screen
project into me, to see my sadness

shine into a searcher's hopeful panic.
They would love me for living, at that moment,
in a shape they once fit, their own story

of loving too much what they had to lose
burnished by the distant confidence of age.
Yet my boredom remained unwritten . . .

(The first trail of hurt and I had lost it
as the woman, whom I loved, would say to me
as to an emptiness, *you have lost me.*)

The twilit streets narrowed to a funnel
drawing me through the hours
to an air-conditioned residence inside myself

with a bean bag chair and a TV showing snow.
And through self-knowing's static I could almost see
how the dog, gone forever, conjured up me—

Masterlove, Good-feeder, now mere *Boy-with-Hands*
shifting gears beyond town limits
where no one might call out my name.

Art Pepper

Scared boy, he even fled a cloud
reminding him of what might happen

when his father returned from sea,
wasted, to find him perhaps again

locked out in the cold, waiting
for other drinkers to come home

(his mother, her lover)—the catalysis
of routine violence passing close

like a storm cloud insisting rain;
until the rain did fall

and the father left, returning though
once with a clarinet . . .

And when the cloud came back
in the sound of a memory

the boy had grown, had learned
to let it swell into the note

he now holds in me

as a laser reads his tone
mastered for fidelity—

sweet prismatic splinter and
swing, a double-timing scrape

aiming for my ear
alone in a rented chamber.

Nowhere,
            and I'm with him,

fully in tune as if he stood
hot before me, his life

seeming no more dear to him
than the sax he hawked

for any kind of syrup
he hoped might creep into his heart

like fucked-up love that felt like love
in the belly meadow warmth of his measured joy.

Hungry Art, Art of wind,
of lips upon the reed;

Art of blue, foolish Art,
would you be so nice to come home to?—

Bragging his genius
for a time turned rancid in San Quentin,

swaggering with a ripped-off thuggery honor
and sick with the terror of not seeming criminal . . .

White man junky thief
whose skin glowed narco-green

with the sound of Keats
amped through Pound

I repeat his name

jacked-in to the straight
blowing of a life

clarifying
like butter over flame:

what's home, where's harm;
how to fix; how praise—

Lover, come back to me.
Why are we afraid?

Island

Of course it happened on the Island
where you spent your summer each year

and do so still, the source of fantasy
and old battles real enough they seem to live on,

even after so many who would go
are gone, grown, or down there somewhere

beneath feet happy to trace trail blaze
leading from peak to cove to dilapidated

lobsterman's shack (he rowing his children
everyday to school), the blacksmith's shop,

the quarry slide worked by Italian immigrants,
back to the house the shepherd built

who, legend says, afforded it by pilfering
the captain's safe on a ship harboring from storm:

a path of anecdotes more hidden with each year,
yet reaching further with each year's small adventure—

but where do we follow a history disappearing
on the mainland, so far from this wooded isolate

memory machine activating the senses
until once again you're the moment's maestro

brimming with Spielbergian operatics
composed by ghosts and set to a mental soundtrack?

Something like fear's overture in that pocket of *usness*,
I heard it then, it claimed me in no exaggerated form;

you were oblivious, keyed to the wind,
the rock, the smell of salt, my smell

mixing with yours shining us
forward so fast I turned a corner despite the past

or because of it—standing on some granite
and looking out at all the other islands

confronting the Island, didn't I choose
when I asked you? And when you said *Okay. Yes,*

did you imagine the bolt of wind winding around us
sang a mysterious sounding chorus

for the story being written now, this current
more powerful even in its calm pulling

past islands the telescope can't see
than we who would be its writers?

As if we were its writers, and love
took shape like a syllable from the mouth.

The Not-Yet Child

Why won't you make me now who wants a life
Inside your life?
                    I fear you as a thief

Stealing about the orchards of my future,
Green fruit glistening above a starving creature.

To increase the coin buried inside yourself
You need exchange it for an alien wealth.

Wealth being you? I need to spend my hoard
On public conquests of a private world:
Take drugs and chances, love recklessly, and build.

I promise I'm your most famous bright adventure.
My stanzas will collapse, mere rooms in nature . . .

I understand: you dwell on agony;
But there you'll shape your strongest poem, me.

Your cry will play the tune ending my work
As health plays boss over the art I serve.

Not always helpless, some day I'll help you,
And you'll be grateful for what I give to you.

Fever, high blood pressure, and sleeplessness?
I've my beloved to cause me such distress,

And in my distress I find again denial—
If I'm the father how can I stay the child?

*Make me, and as your face grows old
You'll find in my face your face taking hold.*

That's vanity you call posterity.
Afraid the future bears what you want to see?

Of what I could become but might not be.

Lines to Stitch Inside a Child's Pocket

Boy now, man later; and all the story in between:
Yes breaking down to *No,* joy to pain.

Milk now, meat later; separation, fuse.
Swim the river rising and with patience take your aim.

Miss once, miss again; and your whole life seems a waste.
The target is yourself becoming brave.

Who soon, who later?—whatever happens next—
Someday you'll lose us in the in-between.

The World's Room

Big Meat Fur Teeth
Picks me up, puts me down

Do it do it
DO IT NOW

Dada Doggy
Puppet God

He will, he won't
The floor is cold

I hunt my Milk Song
She: titted sweet for me

Tongue in, tongue out

Mr. Mister
I can sniff him

at the house-hole
wagging bye-bye

Bye-bye, why, high
Hey where, hey how

A door, a page
Both swing first word

Hullo, I said it
Hullo, hear it?

They hear it, they
heard me, it grows to
the room we're in

Next page, please turn

Do it do it
DO IT NOW

She will, she won't
Why. Try. My. Cry
I'll find a shape

Tongue in, tongue out

And be that shape
I make obey me

I love it, Big Meat:
Warm Arm; I love it
Once me: Milk Song

The page opens
A phone opens too

I'll turn it on
And walk right through

Next page, please turn

Do it do it
DO IT NOW

I'm in the page
And now I'm gone.

Nursery Rhyme

Once stood a field of wheat before the rain,
a field of secrets too, and fence knocked down.
Outside the house there is an inside room.

The window cracked for fear that it would change;
the window disappeared (and that was strange).
The window stayed the same and that was change.

Who ate the wheat and burned the fields to black?
The secret bird flew north and can't fly back.
The song inside an ear once filled an emptiness.

That was before the secret bird flew back.
How do we know the secret bird flew back?
The window stayed the same and that was change.

Rain, sleep, and rain is filling up the cup.
A fence of wheat stands still, and still won't stop.
Its breath inside your ear spills from an emptiness.

The opened window calls the children in;
the children fly to kiss their secret friend.
Outside the house there is an inside room.

Plot

Weeks before I worked the site
    I saw myself a carpenter, and practiced pounding
        three-inch vinyl coated sinkers—just nails to me then—
            into a giant wood block until it splintered.

The cross-hatched heads of each nail bent
    accused me of knowing nothing
        I pretended to know, as the sparks that fled
            my hammer glancing off the crippled metal

winked at me in my escapade: *Dear Child of Books,*
    can't you show one callous on your hand?
        I read manuals at night I couldn't understand
            and traced diagrams to lose myself

in mental drafting more like fantasy:
    how the house would rise above me,
        my precocious mastery of craft
            so impressing the carpenters

they would all chip in for a leather tool belt,
    buy me beers and run their fingers
        down a seamless joint, declaring
            my apprenticeship was done.

First day I brought my hammer
    Mark borrowed it, led me to a scrubby plot, said
        Try cutting this down, and left to hammer a nearby house.
            From where I stood the new shining claw

fit so well in his toughened hand
    it was his hand, which he waved to me
        as I picked up the saw, ripped
            the cord and revved it, holding tight

like a zoologist might grasp a strange bird's legs,
    and stepped into the brush, machine teeth
        racing and spitting to bite and spew
            green wood flesh, dead limbs, debris.

Goggles fogging, boots unsure against the steep
    crumbling grade, I gripped my knees and toes
        into the hillside and silently sang
            to the accompaniment of saw:

how I would conquer the hill and bury all doubt
    that I could manage my tools, my body
        warming to the task, satisfaction risen into pride
            as I razed a square of nature for a job.

Third day, Mark said *Slope's too big for a CAT;*
    so I cleared the lot and started digging
        the foundation with a pick. The dirt was like rock.
            Another laborer and I jack-hammered for a week.

Mechanical pneumatics a kind of sex game
    for the mind set loose by the body's effort,
        he'd lean against the shaking chisel,
            compressed air driving the bit deeper as he pushed,

the work's percussion like some tribal tune.
    He'd pause and smile, *Feels just like a woman.*
        For him, the hole he dug became a piece of art—
            just beautiful, he'd ponder it, examining

its depth, the sharp cut angles and even planes.
　　On paper you could read its purpose,
　　　　but the hole's meaning deepened for us,
　　　　　　the makers of the hole, beyond its first significance;

until the hole became a word
　　repeated into senselessness: dumb hole, dada hole,
　　　　the two of us working in it for hours by ourselves,
　　　　　　our one intimacy, a point of understanding.

Two weeks later I left the job
　　blistering everywhere with poison oak.
　　　　I took colloidal oatmeal baths
　　　　　　and mixed a hoo-doo paste

to soothe the raw bubbled skin around my eyes
　　and genitals. Apprenticeship barely begun,
　　　　I had succumbed to the weakness of my own system,
　　　　　　and labored to conjure this most

recent version of myself
　　draining away like water from an itching body:
　　　　I dreamed of black sap
　　　　　　oozing from extension cords exposed to rain,

the blade's metallic argument, and then
　　the night my grandfather died
　　　　that I shot a man chasing me
　　　　　　down a dark city street. I ran

and ran to my childhood house
    and took apart the gun
        and buried each piece in a separate hole.
           I heard music in the house.

Upstairs I found a woman who spoke
    a language I almost understood.
        We would marry, and when I woke up
           a voice on the phone said *fly to Florida*.

I understand now why I dug the hole:
    to build a house you need a hole.
        I fell in love with the music of the work
           and made up words to sing along—

a hammer, a gun, both make a song;
    but who was the man chasing after me
        or the woman who would claim my life
           in a foreign tongue? The joints won't show

and now the labor is done. And not having ever seen the house
    I am left with a hole like a word without a thing,
        while Mark, who always took time
           to unroll the plans so I could try to follow,

traces the lines from the architect's plot
    to strings pulled tight above the ground
        to an imaginary point in space
           he sees the house will reach.

Market Day

Old man and deaf
again bends over late afternoon's
ever-growing mound of culls—

split melons, thumbed peach, berries
sweaty and bleeding to the touch,
and all the musty burdock, turnip,

shrinking beet and jicama—picking the sweet
spoils of heat and accident
with deliberation. His face turned away

it seems impossible he could sense me
tugging the loaded produce cart
through the store's aisled back

barracks of food, stacks crowded
beneath twitching fluorescence,
but he turns as I turn

the corner towards him and smiles
sheepish and confident. He seems to balance
the embarrassment of his bad hip with a cocky

hat tilt, one hand raised to say hello
and hold me from my obligatory scolding:
You can't be back here—workers only.

Random as a familiar dream, he
is sudden, unexpected, yet known—
another shapeless day of repetition

in my kingdom of fruits and vegetables
now his day, made distinct with his poise
and his need. Once I watched him slip a granola bar

into his baggy torn pants. He knew
I had seen him, and he grinned at me
so fiercely, so impressed

with his own cheap cunning
I wanted to knock him down,
take away his prize and eat it.

And yet if he never showed again
I wouldn't miss him in this foodscape,
with its regulations and more than one

tight-ass manager to tell me
keep it straight; I might wonder
after a while if he had moved

or died or found a better deal,
but only for a moment, caught up
in the procedures of kindness

I enter into every day
as I pick out the ripest, cut off a taste,
aware always of the clock and my wage.

He hands me a pad to scribble
'free' on and sign, his slight routine bow
in response made grudgingly,

a kind of payment, then gathers the bags
found and filled from earlier rounds, other stores,
and limps toward the front floor

past the rack dripping with the day's fresh retail,
in each grimace, each halting step
the effort of it all revealed and hidden.

Who They Were

Thanksgiving day, no one yet thinks of him
as dead, his loneliness a new career
with which he seems preoccupied and proud.
Eyes tracing us at lunch, the cane he hates
still gripped while sitting, he's all quiet cheer,
a cartoon smile beneath a rheumy stare
absorbing family pomp and the pitch
of conversation teasing him like slang
he sometimes understood. He plays his brow
like a signal flag so we can see he's there.
Assured and brainy, even now, he begins to speak
deliberate roping sentences that coil
off the spool of stories spinning in his head:
how Uncle Doc, a plumber struck by lightning,
took care of two Jew-haters on the subway
by slamming heads together in a brawling kiss,
then hauling them like beaten luggage curbside
and stealing their cigars;—or he sees himself
a boy in Russia prior to the coup,
holding his mother's keys as she is shot
for running guns to Lenin . . .

                                   Was it true
or merely true enough?

Desperate to snare
some history late in middle age, my mother,
prepared with tape machine, holds out the mike:
Say it again Dad, speak into the thing.
He laughs and shakes his head, sips once and sighs,
the heaving past calm now beneath the surface
of everything he'd like to say, and shy
before posterity's cool instruments.

. . .

Another year, a stroke, yet still he is here;
speaks less; sings opera when the pizza comes.
He smiles at his son and recognizes me
but not my name or who I am: *grandson:*
a future pale as the once prized heirlooms
cramping his apartment, and as unknown.
Two portraits bordered with gilt above his bed:
his mother and father, stiff in formal dress,
stern, regal, staring beyond revolution
to the Soviet Union they would never see
or see their son escape from. His stare back
falls blunt, yet he sees there is some relation:
aunt, brother, cousins from a distant farm?
Who they were, failed to be, or might have been
fades from the dream-talk of his memory
until the frame itself begins to crack;
so that gazing at them he is like: Aeneas
scanning with wonder the images engraved
on Vulcan's shield—they could be children unborn
forecast in pictures, all their destined acts
hanging beyond the mind like a hemorrhage.

Hoisting a bright wool afghan to his shoulder,
lips pressed and flakes of scalp dusting his stoop,
he trembles, scowling, steel-eyed and aroused
for battle, ready to walk through a field
full-blown with bodies and sing out to the tribe.

Mongrel Death Blues

What's that behind my back?
What's that gnawing behind my back?

It sounds like a dog crunching bones for marrow.
Bones here so old, the sun's dried up the marrow.
What kind of dog splinters bone like that?

Don't turn around, I hear it getting louder.
Don't turn, don't turn, its growl is getting louder.
Oh, don't you growl at me, nappy rabid dog.

My joints may be cracking, but my bones ain't buried yet.
I said, my skeleton is talking, but my bones ain't buried yet.
Hear my belly growling? I'm hungrier than I've ever been.

Are you baring pearly whites? I can almost smell your mongrel breath.
Yes, your pearlies, they are snapping, and I can smell your stinking breath.
I'd turn around and pet you, but I've given up on pets.

I am reaching for a stone.

I swear my aim is sharp.
I swear my arm is strong.

It's growing dark, but I won't miss.
It's darker now, but I won't miss.
O shine down moonlight, my whole life has led to this.

The Visitation

Before he died he saw a vision
    Of my grandmother in the kitchen
Determined in her evening dress.
    She asked him if he cared to dance—

'My handsome Sam, come make your heart stronger.'
    But he said 'No, making soup right now,
Your recipe, a little altered
    By Esther, the good-looking one next-door.'

'My handsome Sam, I watch you wander
    Our apartment all alone;
What kind of life when the TV talks
    And you talk back to a thing you own?'

'Don't get ideas, I'll follow you shortly,
    I'm making a pot of soup right now,
And our boy Mervyn will be calling—
    I have to be here to pick up the phone.'

She disappeared, came back naked,
    The girl of twenty the day they met
When he walked off the boat from Russia
    And she combed lice off his greasy head.

'You don't give up easy, never did—
        Reminds me of our wedding night.
I was so happy when we married.
        My soup is cool enough to eat now.'

'Eat your soup Sam, and take your pills,
        And talk to Mervyn on the phone,
And when you feel your heart hang up
        You'll be with me, but without a home.'

In the apartment we find their letters,
        Books about sex, the Diaspora story;
We eat some soup, and I talk on the phone
        To the woman I once thought I'd marry.

Epitaph

He can't remember what they bought,
two corner mausoleum plots or two
in the center, but he doesn't trust
those bastards, they'll take
your money and who knows what,
he wants to go back, watch
the deposit, make sure he gets what he paid for—
he wants the right spot, the one they picked out
together, *not* in the corner, in the *center,*
because they planned it all, and with his heart
he was going to die first,
and she'd remember where to put him.

The Knife

Even when speaking of alien things
the poet speaks his own language.
— BAKHTIN

Knife, etymology uncertain.

As a knife it attracts me: 11 inches, 11 ounces, it fits firmly in the hand. The flat top edge invites my thumb to rest there, even give it a little rub, while my index finger tucks into the stem curling like a comma from the hilt, to keep the hand in place while thrusting. A long indelible smudge marking each side of the blade suddenly stops, as if the knife had been stuck into something and—regretfully?—pulled out. As if it couldn't go any further.

The knife is a single piece of steel, the dark plastic sandwiching the handle kept in place on either side by two pins, the heads of which shine like eyes hardened into beads. Sweat has worn the metal surface, particularly where the fourth and fifth finger wrap around the end. Its sheath is black metal and fits snug as a condom. Handsome and sinister, like a man in a cloak in a cloak-and-dagger thriller, its reality denies fiction, conjuring myth in the shape of history instead. The knife *is* history, or rather, summons history, as, on the blade itself, beneath the circled initials stamped by the manufacturer, *RZ,* and the model number, *M7/72,* reads the date, *1940.* And on the handle, embedded in the plastic, a swastika sits on a diamond-shaped background of minutely dimpled ruby and a clean flat white.

Did my grandfather, a paratrooper during the war, buy it from a comrade selling collected spoils, or did he take it himself off a corpse he found or— . . . ?

In my hand now the steel absorbs my heat, leaving in turn a metallic smell on my skin. The cutting edge is still keen—you could shave with it—and you can see where a sharpening stone has worn the edge to renew the bevel. Perhaps my grandfather even sharpened it himself well into the night forty years later in a Florida condo. And dreamed of what?—Its original owner, some sweet young man with a passion for philology, or a dumb hulking cliché of sadism, or any boy, really, with a little sugar for the fatherland? The knife passes hands in darkness, settles in my grandfather's hands in darkness. How many died by the knife? I mean, by this knife? Perhaps no one, perhaps the only meat it touched was an occasional bird stolen from a farm. (*Perhaps, perhaps:* a self-conscious refrain in the mouths of children seeking—avoiding—the shaded avenues, their deeper shadows).

—Where reality, fiction, myth, history (such abstractions!) fit together like bricks in a wall, the wall a poem standing in a city I know I'll never find. *Even when speaking of alien things, the poet speaks his own language*—meaning, the poet's voice is only his own, and what enters it becomes his own and cannot be known as other. Quoting Whitman, the knife mocks, *I too am untranslatable,* driving me to find someone who can prize such a thing so charged with the infinite possibility of an unknown and unknowable past it induces nausea; but I cannot sell it for fear that it will find its way into the wrong hands. (Or, depending on your politics, the right hands). So I will keep it now though I do not want it, its heavy muteness refuting the poem I cannot write about the knife, that is a poem of secret eloquence against my work.

Riddle Book to the City

I am announced like thunder
from the hand of God, yet remain
impartial. Justice? Who cares.
I wait to feel my master's coaxing
finger, the fire wasp seeking
a hive of flesh. When I find my love
I burrow to daylight or the city's electric night.
Men have survived me, even children,
even fools!—but not without strife
and some wonder at my can-do
to damage what I keep my eye on.
Lost, I fall to earth,
but even in my aimless slumber
I've been known to take a life.
How can you legislate my rest
when so many who would curse me
secretly wish me in their camp?
Friend or foe, can you name me
before I find my Jerusalem
in your body or a body that you love?

2.

Inside the neon cave: a mocking
carnival of bodies endlessly combined,

false budding semblances to dim the mind
for you, who want them. And for you who don't:
this reminder of your brother's appetite.

3.

Pea-brained angelics of the city,
we leave our markings randomly
on sidewalk, windshield, or bouffant.
Our music is the sound of fondness,
the low appreciative compliant patter
of those dependent on the scraps of others.
When you guess our name, you'll hear it pinched
as the pockets of your nesting
we hide ourselves in:
stout, short of leg, but capable
of taking off, at least, with something like grace.

4.

A world adorned with unworldly logic,
the city's ornaments are diverse and strange—
these uniform contraptions pulsing
through the arteries, a navy of corpuscles
pumped from the invisible muscle of need:
to already be there, to get away . . .

We travel without route, improvising
among the green to red to green
of late afternoon's clotting catastrophe.
Declaring our presence with a sea lion's temper
we seem blind to each other's dangers, speeding
along what doubles as a roof
for those who live beneath the solid stream of tar.
Even cheap poets have called out in the rain,

hoping (of course!) to be seen
or heard by one of us, bright ship
harboring in motion till it hears its name.
Poet or not, can you guess what
hums inside the city seeking you,
late to the next somewhere
it's so important for you to be?

(bullet, porn shop, pigeon, taxi)

Connecting Flight

Late to my gate, still
I feel in control, light,
with just a canvas bag
slung messenger-fashion
round my neck and across
my chest; thus my arms
move freely, help pump
me forward, balance, negotiate
the encumbered crowd, even
hold a coffee. I'm feeling cocky,
duck into a newsstand
and squat to gaze greedily
at a bottom row of magazines.
When I see him
coming down the concourse
with obvious effort, each hand hooked
on a heavy bag's grip, fingers white,
squeezed bloodless by the weight,
neck tendons taut with strain,
despite the years I know his face
aged terribly in dreamtime,
jowl peppered red with his college
shaving rash, and a scrubby rug up top
to punctuate an anxious scowl.
God, he scowled with a wit
I loved, even turned against me,

until, what happened?—the mysterious
betrayal, his refusal, his silence—
I want to rise up
and denounce him, who was once
like a brother, turn the airport
into a court for killed friendship;
but the cashier shakes her head—
sorry, not policy, no can-do, hands tied . . .
I follow him without a sound, weaving
and dodging like swimming
through the mass, overtake him,
move past, out the gate, down the steps,
to wait by the plane. Am I a dog?
Outside it's lovely, even the engines.
He approaches, puts the bags
(with relief) at my feet, hands me
his pass without recognition.
Joey. But he's on the plane now
(how did he board without climbing the stairs?)
the plane already climbing,
then seeming to pause
to accent a cloud.
A smiling steward touches my arm
and shouts to the all-around whine.
Is he singing or speaking?
What are the words?
He points to the plane; he points
to the bags, my hands
locked on leather handles
still moist from those hands . . .

Tempest

Three thousand miles from this outermost seaside province,
  sky darkening to a purple amber wash across the harbor,
you, Crispus Sallustius, sit in your house perched among hills
  of a western paradise, and consult with your lawyer how best
to sue my ass. Lift your pen from the page and look out your window,
  how the heavy light seeks the world and warms it,
drying the sodden earth and seducing reluctant buds.

Just weeks ago, rain that never stopped, would never stop, it seemed,
  attacked the panes like buckshot flying sideways with the wind:
bad news in the mail, phone, fax, online; your enemies'
  triple-headed barking on a river-edge brimmed over
plosive and cascading, the river of your ire strangling by submerging,
  as dreams too filled up with rain, and banks refused to hold.
But here, as there (despite all precipitation) the rain's rained out,

while salt air and sun yank the covers off and lick us to rise up
  and hum;—why waste your precious coins and minutes
on battle plans for some official dim interior, the polished wood
  and balustrade reflecting back in brass our convexed likenesses
as we prevail upon dignitary robes to judge us, who cannot sit still in silence.
  What could satisfy your hunger? The starving adventurer, having wandered
lost in mountains drenched by rain, falls on a shepherd's humble table,

and eats until he's sick, chucks it up to force it down, belly in revolt
  against an agitated mind. Agitated to anger at my mere figure on your step—

you shouldn't have come here; you're responsible, you owe—
   carbon pupils flaring, oh how I *fucked you over, over good*
as I stood wooden and bewildered, lost in panic's wood,
   and you gathered breath to bellow like an actor on his final stage
overcome, for the finish, by black fury's torrent finding its voice

merging with your own, your doubled voice enriched
   as a venting pleasure frothing over under all around
carried me off in a ripping ugly rush *I'm not your father, your keeper*—
   . . . Well, I couldn't have agreed more; though months later
I'd reverse that if I saw you now, and try (no doubt failing)
   to bow to you, my . . . *keeper,* so close this long winter
I too gorged myself on platters of revenge

and tart sorbets kept cold in a metal dish of fear . . .
   Nights of reverie at the sink, each plate congealed with meat juice
a model of my mind I tried scrubbing and scrubbing smooth;
   or was I just a fool, my mind more water pouring from the faucet,
seeking the basin to give it shape, contain it, yet finding only drain
   and a polluted route to other larger waters?
Does your epic of triumph and suffering need this minor book?

Take your pen to a blank page of scrap, boot up
   and delete my name from your data bank. You have others to care for
without taking care of me, our fates mixed together makes more stormy weather,
   and see, it's just stopped raining . . . So step to your balcony
and breathe the new atmosphere thoroughly cleaned of me—
   that's life! egging your heartbeat on. I want more of it too than could ever fill
         me up,
before the rain falls again (this time falling with no end) late season's

   floodwater sweeping out our cherished homes.

Oakland 1991

Distant smoking
  ribbons rising
from brown hills;
  echo of steam
twirling off the burnt
  black pond
of day's first coffee
  in cups we cupped
to drink from hot.
  October heat
like summer, everything
  parched but wild
fennel reaching
  higher than a boy,
conquering concrete
  to beckon you
break off a sprig
  for finger scent,
no need to bend
  over, and the soft
snow of cinders
  starting to add up.
Sirens distant,
  drifting high
in a muddy smudging
  sky to circle

down closer now,
    now here
like the voice of a pissed
    B-actress with just
one line, and soon
    jamming my ear
with fire as flames
    take over
nearby homes:
    (*ham; koiman:* bed)
those put to sleep
    beneath Olmsted's
cemetery
    also bearing heat
just a block away
    kid with blinking
lights in his hightops
    says—he's staying!—
fuck the 'rents
    loading up, anxious
to join the stream
    of headlights shining
through daytime
    twilight of ash
falling, the sun
    eclipsed by smoke,
ashes smeared on
    windshield while
generations of fires
    turning mornings
first burning to
    increase insensible,

nature in passage
    that *desireth*
and requereth alwey
    jumping the fire line
so what good's the line
    like a need grown
godly in petulance,
    mind in shaking
fever feeding
    on dreams & figments
of disease, or a nation,
    or a love confused
by immolation . . .
    Forget the stuff,
let's hit it —
    grabbing *The Dynasts*
(first edition,
    one volume
complete, 1910)
    a disk, a photo
(my grandfather,
    Bar Mitzvah, Russia,
1910) a poem
    in draft, my meds,
my stuff, my story;
    though I hoped too,
excitedly, I admit,
    it would all go up
higher than it might,
    like a bug on a current
or a promise
    or a thought,

as I paused there
  (would there still be there?)
at the step, to turn
  the deadbolt shut.

Kindertotenlieder

Not a day ended that the mind did not seek
         a spot in the mind,

tender and dark, bruised by a fear
         finding its shape there,

that neither grew nor deepened, but only ached
         always, reminding

something could, at any moment, sometime
         happen, could happen

as things happened, and they could (and did)
         happen, for example, to anyone—

to his sweet dirt genius, queen prankster, joy bean:
         little girl *kinder,*

bright unafraid millenium's child,
         waking each day

like a sun rising new on the world,
         eager to shine original

and burn it up with attention—the bruise
         of *could happen*

could bloom just like a daydream
                 that takes you in transport

for the long trip's duration
                 as moment by moment

the window frames a new picture
                 (a trip that once started never can end . . .)

Composer obsessed, he stayed on board with it,
                 traveling further

into discolored regions, filling the heart
                 with the heart's bitter juices

—bruise sap, wound gas—to make from his fear
                 of what could, perchance, happen

a cycle of songs on the death of children
                 which deepened the bruise

with the heat of making, his full attention
                 to shaping, to saying,

to singing fiercely what he could not
                 dwell on, or in

until what had not happened
                 rose up a house of song.

And when his wife protested
                 that fate had been tempted,

he had no license to take another man's poems
                    built from real grief

and set them to music,
                    was he crazy

in love with disaster, spoiled by fame,
                    or proving (again)

he was more than some thought him,
                    a frustrated conductor . . .

And when his own daughter died
                    afterward—

after the work was completed,
                    receiving praise

and kisses from friends filled with envy
                    (who loved him more for it);

after he too sat on several occasions,
                    listening again

to hear just how good, rightly made and sung
                    and so deserving

praise, and stood for applause—
                    after all that: accomplishment

burned to ash; and the mind's bruise
                    (the taste of ash all he tasted)

opened its patient, dread primordium
                as if perennial

and long overdue, and he heard
                the songs anew—

a dark magic now, a mocking invocation
                to some god, to God,

to make what was sung true now
                to fact, and scatter

the notes coherent in the ear
                such that his ear

could no longer hear music
                where once it seemed mind

found a contour through sound:
                his songs made this happen.

Now gone beyond our heat we feel you light
                Us with our loss, and we burn bright—

So I wrote on the death of another's boy,
                how they dreamed him a man

Who, in the world, remembered us as well
                And loved us finally,

as we love him still. And still I feel
                the mother's bodily warmth

surprising me with her thankful embrace
        for a poem I wrote

as a kind of professional, carried
        to experience

on *poesy's wing* flapping in strained imitation
        behind the forged weld

between that and this, there and here,
        then and now . . .

Yet I know I felt something, the movie of losing
        what was not mine to lose

entertaining and twisting me all through the night
        as I worked at the page

for right combinations I might steal
        or conceive . . .

And it spoke to her so fresh in her grief,
        as if annihilating sadness

could warm to life such inert manipulations,
        like a golem sparked

by a rebbe's learned and greedy tongue
        (to turn to its maker, and turn on its maker) . . .

And I have a son now—imagination sprung
        grubby and driven—

rising hot from dream-sheets to master
   the world:

truck, pop, water, up,
     block, two, egg, shoe —

though not a day ends that the mind does not seek
    a spot in the mind,

tender and dark, bruised by a fear
     finding its shape there—

Mahler's *Kindertotenlieder* a warning and a question
    I cannot keep from asking,

as this poem also would not stay unwritten,
    my own need for *never*

pulling me to it, as now I sing it
    (now almost sung)—

the poem you hear from my mouth
    to your ear,

will it find further life on some fateful
    tongue called to taste it,

that even now might be wagging
    with ardent incantation,

obscenely coaxing its nightmare
    stalk to bloom?

Bruno's Night

Up the hill of snoring
The father climbs in dream,
The mother sinks in silence
And baby sucks its thumb.

But struggling next door
Boy Bruno smells the dawn
While the sick, the sad, the torn
Apart quiet their song.

Dropped curtains hide the night's
Inspired fantastic pomp
That liquidates with light—
Don't oversleep—Wake up!

Run to the grimy window,
Press your nose to the dirt.
Under the dawn: you follow
The mass of gathering earth.